T0146882

IF **TREES** COULD **TALK**
(WHAT WOULD THEY SAY?)
&
AND THE **WORLD** WAS ...

RUTH M. GLASS

iUniverse®

IF TREES COULD TALK (WHAT WOULD THEY SAY?)
&
AND THE WORLD WAS ...

iUniverse books may be ordered through booksellers or by contacting:

iUniverse
1663 Liberty Drive
Bloomington, IN 47403
www.iuniverse.com
1-800-Authors (1-800-288-4677)

ISBN: 978-1-5320-0364-6 (sc)
ISBN: 978-1-5320-0365-3 (e)

Library of Congress Control Number: 2016914142

Print information available on the last page.

iUniverse rev. date: 09/09/2016

CONTENTS

PART TWO: AND THE WORLD WAS ...

ABOUT THE AUTHOR

Ruth Glass is a native of the state of Arkansas. She moved to Berkeley, California at an early age. Ruth received her education from Laney-Merrill College and also at the Bay Area School of preaching in Oakland, California.

Ruth is the mother of eight children: four sons and four daughters. One son, Shaldon Tavoy is deceased. Her first publications as a poet were in 1980-81 and 1982-83 in **VOICES IN AMERICAN POETRY** under her maiden name, Ruth McMahan.

She is a retiree of J.C. Penney Company. After the death of her husband, she moved to Portland, Oregon where she later met and married Bruce Glass.

Presently, Ruth is an active member of the Northwest African American Writers' Workshop and has published several inspirational poems in the anthology, KUUMBA, which is a yearly publication of the Northwest African American Writers' Workshop.

THE TALKING TREE
MOTTO: USE US BUT DON'T ABUSE US

I'M THE TREE
BY RUTH GLASS

MAN, GOD MADE ME -
AND GOD MADE YOU TOO.
I WAS HAPPY - AND SO WERE YOU.

MAN, YOU DISOBEYED GOD.
YOU ALLOWED YOURSELF TO SIN.
YOU CAUSED THE PUNISHMENT OF DEATH UPON
EVERYTHING, INCLUDING HUMAN - AND THEN;
YOU TOOK MY WOOD AND MADE A CROSS
YOU HUNG GOD'S SON THE SAVIOR FOR THE LOST.
HOW MANY MORE MEN, DID YOU HANG ON THE TREE?
HOW MANY MORE MEN, CRIED PLEASE SET ME FREE?
YOU'VE CAUSED ME SADNESS, AND SHAMELESS OF FACE.
BUT GOD STILL LOVES YOU, AND OFFERS YOU GRACE.

THE TREE

YOU TOOK MY WOOD AND MADE A CROSS

DEDICATION

To my children:
William, Steven, Crystal, Renita, Patrice,
Royce, Shaldon and Joy,
to my parents,
Lorina Harris McMahan and Money McMahan,
and to my husband, Bruce,
my grandchildren and all of my friends.

Love to All of My Children

I love you truly, all of my children.
I love you, I'll love you always.
I love you truly, all of my children.
I'll love you 'til the end of my days.

You were the sweetest little people
That I'd ever seen.
When you entered my life,
You completed my dream.

You've stolen my love
Tho we drifted apart,
But you'll bring me more children
To comfort my heart.

So, now I love you, all of my children
And I love you all of my grands.
I hope to live on for a while
To see how my family expands.

It is a wonderful feeling,
It is beautiful to me
To see my children grown up
And my grands at my knee.

THE TREE CONVENTION

Grass carpeted in and around a large forest where a great number of trees were having a convention. Each kind of tree had several representatives. Their meeting was called to discuss their importance to mankind.

There was a softly running brook nearby, and the sun shone bright like a spot light that seemed to frame the forest like a lovely picture on the face of the clear blue water while the trees went into their discussions.

Palm Tree

The Palm Tree stood tall, straight, and very graceful. It took charge of the great meeting; therefore, the Palm Tree made the first speech. "I am the strongest tree there is, and I am beautiful. I have no wild bent limbs. I can stand the storms and winds. I was famous in the days of Jesus, and I am spoken of in the Bible. No wonder man likes me for shade and beauty." This was the Royal Palm speaking. "Of course, I am also speaking for the Palmettes, Coconut, Dates and Sages Palms which supply man with fruits, waxes and oils. These are very useful products. Yes, besides our evergreen-like beauty, we are also useful. People use our oil to beautify their skin and hair. Some people just can't cook and make their salads without our oil. Oh, my, how we suit their taste. And we trees purify the air they breathe.

THE ORANGE TREE

The next tree to speak was the most beautiful with lovely green leaves and golden round fruit. Yes, it was the Orange Tree. The tree began its speech by saying, "I am the most important citrus fruit that can ever be obtained for the health of man. I speak of the Tangerine, Grapefruit, Limes and Lemons which are a little sour, but they are all members of my family. We are all beautiful and most spectacular when our fruits are ripe. We are so full of good health for children and all mankind."

THE OAK TREE

The Oak Tree took the stand. "I am a very important tree for man. They need my wood for they value it because it is durable for their furniture, home fuel, corks and many other things and products. Oh, yes, they use my bark for tanning and medicines. We are grouped as Black, Red and White Oaks. We produce beautiful green leaves in the spring and little acorn-like nuts. Our leaves are very pretty in the fall. They turn red, golden and brown. Yes, we are one of man's best friends. People travel from far and near to see our beauty. Let us sing the people's well loved song about the tree, 'I think that I shall never see a poem lovely as a TREE,' written by Joyce Kilmer." Then Mr. Oak lifted his voice once more to sing, "I shall not be moved just like a tree planted by the river of waters. I shall not be moved." Mr. Ash Tree was very pleased with Mr. Oak, because the Ash Tree feels closely connected to the Oaks.

THE MAPLE

The Maple Tree speaking very gracefully, stepped forward to proclaim its usage. "I am somewhat like the Oak Trees, but I am one that is classed as an ornamental tree. I am very useful to man. Beside using my wood for their chairs, tables, beds, cabinets and other beautiful furniture, they get syrup from the sap of our Sugar Maples in early spring to satisfy their sweet tooth."

THE RUBBER TREE

The Rubber Tree stretched a bit and bounced to the floor to tell how man gets much pleasure and joy from its products. "Man gets tires for his cars and his bicycles and his airplanes. They make balls and bright balloons for their children, bands for little girls' hair, erasers for their mistakes, and many other products they make for other markets. I am indeed important to man."

THE ENGLISH WALNUT

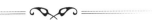

The English Walnut and the Black Walnut trees told of their rich nuts and how lovely furniture is made from their woods. The Pecan and other nut trees also told their stories. "Man loves our oils for tanning." The Almond Tree stood quickly and started to speak, "I must say you know how mankind loves our nuts for their ice cream, cookies, brownies, cakes, pies and candies. They glaze us and chop us to garnish their desserts with our meats. We are really treasured by mankind for their fancy foods." The Banana Tree with its golden and green fruits reaching toward Heaven as they mature and ripen was delighted to tell how mankind eats bananas daily for their health and how they make puddings, breads and fillings for their goodies. The Plum Tree and Figs told of their good fruit usage, too.

cedar

Douglas fir

The Willows and Wonderful Fruit Trees

The Weeping Willow and other Willows swayed rhythmically with the wind as they made their speeches. The Peach Trees told of their delightful fruits of different kinds and taste: the sweet, juicy Alberta Peach, the Indian Peach, the clear stone and others. They were really bragging a tiny bit of how much they are loved by man. "They love us raw, canned, preserved and in peach cobbler -- Wow! We are one of their favorites!"

The Cherry Tree was next to speak. "Well, man not only loves our fresh fruit; they also love cherry pie. They use our bark for medicine and our wood to make costly furniture and other useful products for their gain."

The Apple Tree took its time molding its well-dressed fruit. The Red Delicious apple pointing out the Yellow Delicious, the green apple and the other apple trees as they all stood tall and proud to be of the apple tree family. "Man really couldn't live if he didn't have us. Man says we are 100% good for their health. They say, 'An apple a day keeps the doctor away.' That means they have to keep our fruit on hand. Mankind gets most of his juices from all of our fruit trees.

THE ORNAMENTAL TREES AND MANY, MANY OTHERS

There were many other trees to speak for their groups. They all told their stories of how they make man happy. Even the thorn tree spoke of its beauty in spite of not being too popular for man. "But it will do for fuel."

There were beautiful flowering Trees in many colors looking their best at the convention. In fact, this was the best convention the trees ever had. Finally, they came to the close of their meeting.

The Palm Tree in charge asked if one of the Cedars would make the closing remarks. The ornamental family of trees stood as one of their evergreens took the stand. Their aroma of their fragrant oils filled the air.

The Cedar on the stage bowed and thanked all the trees for attending this convention. "We, as your ornamental trees, Christmas trees and various Junipers, all say thank you again. Now Mr. Pine will lead us in our tree song for our closing."

They all joined in a circle dancing and singing, while the wind played soft music through their leaves, and the brooks of water ran quietly and smoothly near by. Even the birds kept silent and listed to the trees singing their song. The trees truly had a glorious celebration and had now come to their Grand Finale.

apple

willow

THE TREE SONG

Oh, I'm happy to be a tree.
Man couldn't live if he didn't have me
I bear fruits and nuts for his food.
I fit his every mood.

He builds his house, makes furniture, too.
Without the tree, what would he do?
I'm his medicines and his tea.
I'm his beauty, and his shade tree.

He builds his fence and his boat.
He carves and he cuts 'til he makes me float.
I'm his toothpick, match and beam.
I'm the star of his dream.

So, I'm happy to be a tree.
Man couldn't live if he didn't have me.
I'm his firewood and his food.
I fit into his every mood.

IF TREES COULD TALK TO MAN

It pleases me that you built your house.
There you live with your children and your spouse.
I'm your chair by day,
Your bed by night.
Sometimes, I'm your fire,
And your lamp to give light.
You make me your table to hold your food.
You sand, paint and polish to suit your mood.
I adore the attention that you give.
I'll be your thrill as long as you live.

THE TREE AS A FRIEND

Could you ever find as dear a friend
As a tree to soothe the mind of men?
They carve the likeness of every creature.
Man carves his face and all his features.
He makes statues both big and small,
Wooden dolls; short and tall.
He uses the tree to calm his nerves.
Some even carve a god to serve.
He uses the tree as a good luck charm.
The tree to man is like his right arm.

THE TREE

The wind plays music thru their leaves.
The birds perch on their limbs with ease.
Sometimes the birds will build their nest.
They lay their eggs. You know the rest.
When the baby birds begin to sing,
The wind whistles thru the trees,
"It's Spring."

Falling Leaves

The leaves are falling,
The leaves are falling.
I can hear the seasons calling.
"It's Fall again, it's Fall again,
We can see the beauty of Fall again."

The falling leaves from the trees
Are red, green, tan and gold.
There are oranges of different shades,
Their colors are bright and bold.

People travel from far and near
To see the leaves parade.
It marks the fair of Fall,
A beautiful season, God has made.

The Oak leaves win the trophy.
Osark Mountains take the scene,
With its beautiful falling leaves
Showing the beauty of nature's supreme.

BEAUTIFUL TREES

Who can call all the trees by name,
See their beauty as one and the same.
Trees have families' character and traits,
Like people they give, and also have fate.
There are so many trees - shapes, sizes and heights,
Thin, thick, course and smooth bark, that covers them right.
Their leaves and their needles drape them over with care.
Their lovely color, their fragrance of flowers
And fruits that they bear.
To man, trees are awesome, a magnificent scene.
The trees can capture man's very being.
We are happy to be beautiful trees.
God made us and man is pleased.

TREES, TREES, TREES

We were in the garden, before Adam and Eve.
We were bearing fruits for them to receive.
Just one they were not to eat of, nor touch,
God had warned them of death,
Because He loved them so much.
But Satan stepped in with his lie,
Saying to Eve,
"You can eat of the tree"
And telling her why.
Yes, the fruit of the tree made them wise.
They both were naked, they realized.
So man's first clothing was made with our fig leaves.
For they had hid themselves among the trees.
So we trees have been with you
From the first, we do believe.
We trees purify the very air that you breathe!

Be Thankful for the Tree

Man, did you thank God
That he made me?
The sight of me makes you feel free.
You shape me into a bat, to hit your balls.
You make some large and some are small.
You make so many sticks that I can't name.
But there is one you call a walking cane.
For all my uses, you relate,
Your billy clubs are used in every state.
Oh, I'm so elated to be a tree!
Aren't you thankful that I'll always be?
For no matter what you think, or do,
We trees were here even before
God made you!

A Tree? How Needed!

I'm needed. I'm needed.
I like the sound of that ring!
Man cuts my wood into everything.
Toys, toys - little wagons, cars and trains,
ABC blocks, doll houses and planes.
He uses my saw dust to make man-made wood.
He presses and molds it as only man could.
He makes it look so perfect, it can fool a few.
Pressed wood they call it, and it's durable, too.
With my chips and bark he decorates his yard.
I tell you, the tree is man's trump card!
I could keep on talking about man and the tree.
There would be no man if
There was no me!

The Trees' Prayer

If trees could bow and say a prayer,
They would thank God for his loving care
For being a tree upon this land,
For all our use and help to man.
We are thankful that we'll always be a tree,
Man can never get rid of me.
He preserves our beauty with his shellac.
We play a part in his every act.
Yes, I'm thankful to be a tree,
Man is so in love with me.

PART TWO

AND THE WORLD WAS ...

In the beginning, God created the heaven and earth.

Can you see, my dear friend, what a day it must have been when the Lord God of Gods decided to create? All he had to do was speak. This world was all darkness and without form.

But there were waters around.

For God's spirit moved upon the faces of the waters. And with his giant hands, opened wide, God began to speak and to divide. "First," he said, "Let there be light." And there was light.

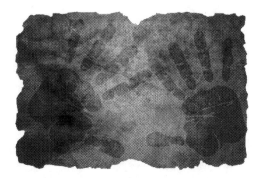

He divided the darkness from the light. He called the light day and the darkness night.

This was the first day, and God said, "This is good."

On the second day, God began to speak to the waters. The waters divided and there was the sky. Now, there was water on earth and water on high. He called the sky Heaven and said "This is good."

The third day, God spoke again and said, "Let the waters be gathered into one place, and let dry land take the other space. He called the waters seas and the dry land earth.

He called for the earth to bring forth grass, herbs, and fruits trees.

Each having its own seed. They all came forth, even the weed.

And God said, "This is good."

On the fourth day, God said, "Let there be light in the heavens." The greater light, the sun, ruled the day.

Greater light and lesser light to rule the night. This was the moon and stars.

And God said, "This is good."

The fifth day, God said, "Let the waters bring forth living things: all kinds of fish and the great whale."

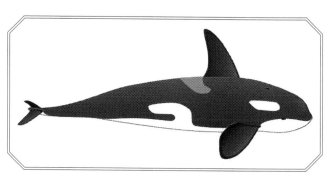

Killer whale

"Let them be both male and female." He made the birds to fly in the sky above, such creatures as the humble dove.

Morning Dove

God blessed them all, saying, "Be fruitful
and multiply, for this is good."

The sixth day, oh, what a busy day. God had no time for play. He told the earth, "You are to bear. Bring forth cattle, beasts and creeping things." Some had wings.

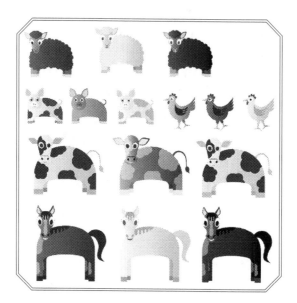

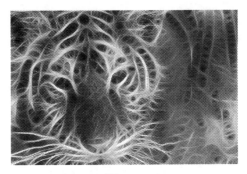

Tiger

Snow leopard

Snake

And God said, "This is good."

Now, deciding that his creatures needed a caretaker, God said, "Let us make man in the image of his Maker."

He shaped the dust of the earth with His hand. That's how God made man. He breathed into his nostril the breath of life, and man's soul became alive. Later God said, "This man needs a helpmate." And so woman he did create.

And God said, "This is good. This is good. This is good."

I AM THAT I AM

Ex. 3:14, Rev. 1:17, 22:13

I am your Captain,
I am King, I am master,
I am your friend.
I am Creator of waters and seas, oceans,
lands and gentle breeze,
rocks, sand, flowers, woman and man,
herbs, fruits and the wind that expands.
I made the trees and the birds that sing.
I made the whole body, including the brain.
I made every color more than you can name.
I made the sun and the sky that man can't frame.
I made every living thing in sight that
you hate or love so much.
I made the wild animals, the tame and the in-betweens.
I created all that's in this scene.
Then I gave man knowledge to work with his hands,
to use his mind and to explore his reign.
Man has a choice to do his will.
Be kind and thoughtful or to be evil and kill.
But I am the one to be heard.
I am the one that has the last word.

I am that I am is the supreme.
"I am" is the fabric of our dream.
"I am" is in charge of the universe.
"I am" is last and
"I am" is
first.

AUTHOR'S NOTE

I am praising the tree as I think they would praise themselves if they could talk. I think they would boast or brag a bit about their all importance to us. They heard the Creator's voice and came forth on the second day. They purify the air that we breathe. They bear fruits, nuts, berries, oils, sap, juices, and syrup that we make so many products with. Their beautiful wood, leaves, bark, chips, and sawdust become buildings, furniture, medicine, tea, firewood, shade and shelter for most creatures. You name it! The tree is used to make it.

The tree would remind us that the Creator made Man or humans with His hands on the sixth day to be the caretakers of all other creations. When Man woke up, everything was here and in place. The same as today. We are born and wake up one day to find ourselves here. With everything in place already! The tree is Great and so are we. But they can and did live without us–we can not live without them. So, I think they are pleased to be used and not abused!

The tree furnishes us with so much beauty, flowers, charm, and creativity. Yes, I also believe the tree would, by all means, encourage Man to respect the Almighty Creator–The Great Power That No Man Controls–No Knob to Turn–No button to Push– No lever to Pull Up or Down. The age old name for that Great Power is GOD!

Printed in the United States
By Bookmasters